GENTLE MANNERS

A GUIDE TO GOOD MORALS

D0610737

"Nothing on earth is more beloved and honored in the world's great heart, than a noble youth, whose aims are high, and whose life is a moral essay"

CANTERBURY, N.H.

PREFACE TO FIRST EDITION.

The following pages were written by the instructors of the school at New Lebanon, N.Y. who in the course of teaching school have often felt the want of some publication of this kind, suitable for the perusal of youth and children.

They consider it a matter of very great importance that the young mind should be properly and carefully trained up in the right way, not only by example, but by teaching and admonition, and by reading such books as are suitable for them.

They are written in a simple style, adapted to the capacities of young minds; and it is hoped that it may be of real benefit to such youth and children as may have the opportunity of reading this little book.

INSTRUCTORS.

New Lebanon, N.Y.
  February, 1823.

PREFACE TO SECOND EDITION.

The following small collection of instructions was written for the perusal of youth, and such as might think it worth their notice. It is hoped that it may be of real benefit to those who have not had much experience for themselves, and who, like the bee, delight in gathering sweet from every flower.

Although there is generally, no lack of good advice, and when it is dealt out with freedom, it is apt to become burdensome, to many, yet a good remark will never come amiss to those who continually love the pleasant path of wisdom, and who are seeking to fill their minds with that rich treasure of understanding and knowledge, whereby they may shun many needless sorrows and troubles, through this difficult and transient world.

That this little book may do some good, and no hurt, to its readers, and that happiness and prosperity may be their abiding lot, is the sincere wish of the

WRITERS.

New Lebanon, N.Y.
    May, 1844.

In the education of children and youth, and even
of those of more advanced age, there are certain
rules of discipline which should be carefully main-
tained. Our lives are, primarily, for the happiness
of those around us, as well as for ourselves, and the
social relations which we maintain in society, should
impress us with this responsibility. The education
of the mind, so essential for the comfort and pleasure of those with whom we associate, now becomes
an imperative duty. It is the stepping-stone to a
well-ordered Christian life, and harmonizes beautifully with the accepted motto, that, "Order is
heaven's first law."

Following closely upon the above incentive to an
advanced order of association, comes the no less
beautiful quotation,—"Cleanliness is next to God-
liness." Without these angel guides at our right
hand, there might be much greater danger of falling
into temptation.

Salvation in this case comes largely from a disci-
plinary care of the mind and it would be a sad trav-
esty on the name of a gentleman or Christian, to find
that some of the essentials for the foundation of a
better character were carelessly ignored, through a
mere matter of indifference.

Fortunately for the poor, who are forced to earn
their daily bread, as well as for the sick and afflicted,
or even for the aged, there is no cast monopoly, of

the ethics of etiquette. Those who are gathered within what they may term a fashionable circle, may arrange for themselves a code of rules which it might be highly proper for them to maintain. This does not, in the least, have any unpleasant influence upon the general good manners that should prevail among those in the more humble walks of life.

It should be the duty of us all, to study so far as we are able, the rules of propriety, and to maintain, both at home and abroad, a careful reserve while having a thought for our own home and a special thought for the friends around us.

The first edition of this little work, published under the name of "A Juvenile Monitor," was written at New Lebanon, 1823. It was a small book of only twenty pages, but contained some excellent instruction in regard to behavior toward those, elder or younger, as well as in Company,—toward strangers and at the table. It also contained rules for cleanliness, and for general good behavior.

The Second Edition was revised and enlarged by Elder Giles B. Avery, of New Lebanon, N.Y.; and printed at Canterbury, N.H. in May, 1844. It was a 16 mo of 130 pages. It had a general circulation in the Community of Believers, and for several years was used as one of the reading books, in many of the schools.

Since the above date, many changes have taken place in the general manners and customs, in all classes of society, and more care and attention is now given to the better cultivation of the social civilities, and from a better and higher standpoint.

We trust that this little work which has accepted freely, the kind labors of many others, who have thought and written on this subject, may be the means of doing some positive good. If it stimulates an active thought for more careful discipline of the mind, it will have accomplished a worthy object.

Other works, more extended, and beautifully written, having an interest in this same subject, may be consulted by those who wish to become proficient in the "good graces" of well disciplined society.

HENRY C. BLINN.

East Canterbury, N.H.
  March, 1899.

In writing this preface, I do so with trepidation, as following such knowledgeable minds as Elder Giles Avery and Elder Henry Blinn seems unattainable. However, I am proud, with my limited ability, to promote the fourth edition of GENTLE MANNERS.

Since the turn of the century, a certain informality or casualness of living has been the mode. This is acceptable to an extent if we do not forget the nice, thoughtful, courteous way of living. Genteel living and good manners are needed as much today as one hundred years ago, and I would add perhaps more so as the general trend is to live more "naturally". In doing so, the gracious art of gentle, good manners has been neglected.

Children should be taught, from the time they can understand, the basic principles of living together harmoniously. These can be taught through observation of the use of good manners by those around them.

May the reading of the wise counsels and rules of good etiquette herein, be applied to each and everyone's daily life. The instruction of these good manners is important, and when followed, young and old can take their place in society confidently knowing they will be welcomed anywhere.

BERTHA LINDSAY.

Canterbury, N.H.
July, 1978.

CONTENTS.

REFLECTIONS.

It may be quite proper to refer to some things, in conduct and deportment, that in the future may be of special benefit. It is necessary for all children and youth, in order to gain the favor of their elders, the good opinion of their companions, and the love of those who are younger, that they should not transgress the rules of good behavior. That discipline which they have been taught from earlier years, should not be overlooked at any age.

There can be no society nor community without different degrees of rank or superiority. There must be directors, and every individual, as well as every order must have regard to those who stand in advance.

"We often hear from teachers and superiors, and read from books, that we should strive to copy the sayings and doings of those who are elder. But moral teachers and writers do not mean that we should imitate the sayings of the profane, because they appear polished and genteel, or of those who abound in vulgarity, because they are well drest and hold a grade of worldly rank."

"Neither do they wish us to be attracted by those who abound in witty falsehood; or those who are passionate, or proud, or vain. They do not wish us to be attracted to those who scoff at sacred teaching, and ridicule divine things, however, high or imposing the accomplishments of such may be."

"Teachers who counsel us right, would induce us to shun such examples as we would a poisonous reptile. They do not mean that we should regard or look up to those who would lead us by their sayings and doings to disobey good counsel, entice us into habits of dishonesty, intemperance, games of chance, lawless pleasure, extravagance, idleness or any other immoral practice."

"Every friend to youth and virtue would advise us to stand aside from all such persons as far as practicable, and shun such examples: whether produced by the young, the middle-aged, or those more advanced in years."

"They desire that we should copy the sayings of persons whose conversation is refined, simple, pure, chaste and truthful. When persons of steady, sober, temperate habits, act or speak before us to encourage this manner of life, we should give attention, listen and learn: and not only learn but practice."

"All good teachers would have us understand that those who enjoin it upon us to fear God, and be watchful, prayerful, truthful, obedient to good instruction, and to be just and honest, are our friends, to whom we should look with respect and confidence, whose instruction we should ponder and regard. This will prove a shield and defense to us in the hour of trial and temptation."

"Good, moral and spiritual men and women are, or should be, our teachers. Good books are to us true channels of instruction. All these are indispensable; we cannot excel without them. But these are not enough. We must learn by our own observation, and then we shall know how true and important are the things which we are taught. Observe the effect of actions upon mankind."

"We shall see that those who endeavor to live in the light and understanding of moral and spiritual instruction, are as said Jesus,— 'the salt of the earth.' We shall discover that they are the foundation pillars of society; that they are virtuous, and beyond all question, enjoy the satisfaction of well-doing."

"On the other hand we shall see those who are lawless, vicious and unprincipled, never rise to true honor and moral dignity. Passion and appetite always disappoint their worshipers."

EDUCATION.

In the presentation of rules for the guidance of the youthful mind, it may not be out of place to present the following good thought. Good manners demand that we should speak correctly, spell correctly and then write correctly.

The highway to knowledge must be one of the most wonderful, and at the same time, one of the most pleasant places in which to travel, as its beauty becomes more and more resplendent, and the acquisition of its treasures is ever increasing as we move on toward the source of all knowledge, which can be at no other place than in the Holy City of God.

Every step that is taken on this beautiful road should be treasured for the glory of our Father, and for the peace and prosperity of humanity. As our whole lives should be directed toward that which is for the best good of man, we can leave no place for the prostituting of good gifts to a bad use.

In obtaining an education it is quite like the procuring of food and shelter for the body. A half a loaf of bread is much better than none, to the hungry man, and a partial roof over our head, at night, is decidedly better than an exposure to the inclemency of the tempest. So with the poor. A nickel in some instances, proves to be a valuable treasure, and even a penny should not be despised.

We have only to read that beautiful story in the New Testament, of the "two mites," to be assured of the value of a simple offering.

To have learned the alphabet, whether in childhood or in more advanced age, is to have a valuable stepping-stone to the good things beyond that point. With the advantages conferred upon the children, at the present date, very few will be allowed to reach mature age, without having learned this simple lesson.

The alphabet having been committed to memory, next comes the much neglected spelling book. Some teachers have even gone so far as to exclude it from the school room, and pupils are taught to read by words. Any system, however, that will afford the needed instruction, and harmonize with the best writers of the day, will be readily accepted.

Orthography may never become immovably fixed, and this obliges us to accept the changes that may be made in spelling certain words in order to keep pace with the teachers of the English language.

Some have said, that in making a choice between bad spelling and bad writing, they would prefer an article badly written, with good orthography, than an article with nice penmanship and incorrect spelling.

Defective spelling is by no means confined to children, nor to those of limited education. It disfigures the pages of those who have shared the advantages of a liberal education and of many who have been called to instruct others.

If we have the least doubt concerning the formation of a word, we should at once, consult the dictionary and not impose our carelessness upon our correspondents. Some have the habit of writing so badly that it would be quite impossible to determine how the word was spelled, as not more than half of the letters could be deciphered.

As the pupil commences the study of orthography, and that of penmanship at about the same time, he will find that the spelling and writing are very closely conjoined, and the same care should be taken with the formation of each letter while writing, as in marking its correct position in the word.

The story of the young man who solicited the advice of a friend, is to the point. "The young man received a letter from his learned adviser, and for weeks made it his study, as at first he was sanguine that his friend would approve of his scheme. As time passed on, a new light dawned into his mind and he half concluded to abandon the project, but at the same time was diligently studying to decipher the letter."

"He finally progressed so far as to be assured that his legal adviser did not approbate his course. He immediately wrote a reply to the letter, thanking his friend for writing so obscurely, as the effort to decipher the letter had occupied so much time that he had, himself, concluded to proceed no farther with it." In this case the illegible penmanship may have done some good, but we can not commend the course.

It is not kind to send a letter to any one with misspelled words. It publishes the writer, at once, either as an ignorant person or a very careless one. It is certainly improper to consume the time of a correspondent in deciphering poor scrawls of carelessly spelled words.

We know that some words are quite difficult to spell on account of the silent letters, but these words must be clearly impressed upon the mind, or should not be used without special reference to the dictionary.

There are a few simple rules in spelling which may well claim our attention, if we wish to be better informed. To have them so near while we are writing that we can make an easy reference, will save us many blunders, and at the same time save to our friends much precious time.

It has been said, and with much propriety, that a person can not carry two sets of manners. Those that are used at home, when not under inspection, will as a general rule, be used when in company with others.

The same remark will be found true in regard to writing and speaking. The language that we use when about our daily employment, will without doubt, enter into our written articles, and even into the letters that we may write to our dearest friends.

While it may not require much thought to be

able to talk, it does require a careful discipline of the mind to be able to converse, or to write a letter, agreeably, to the rules of English grammar. To use words of doubtful definition, or to use slang, or even words that are not approved in well-disciplined society, is certainly very disrespectful. To be forced to listen or to read the language of a crude or careless person, is sometimes tolerated, but it is far from being appreciated.

FUTURE CONSEQUENCES FROM PRESENT ACTIONS.

Every action must bring its reward of either good or evil. If seed is sown in the earth, it springs up and bears fruit. It matters not whether the time for the fruit be soon or late; the result is equally certain and important.

We may think that little thoughts, words or actions are of no great consequence. How many there have been, who for a time were sincere, and determined to do well, but who, little by little, became entirely changed in their minds and actions! This was done by each particular thought, word or action, though apparently considered at first of little consequence.

He who acts or talks without thinking what he is about, or the consequence thereof, is like one who dashes along, neither knowing nor caring for the dangers he may meet.

When we speak of others, we should be careful to say nothing about them that is disrespectful, or that would tend to their dishonor. Nothing should be reported of them that is not already known, nor should disrespectful comments be made on what is known.

Evil-speaking is ruinous. It scatters and weakens all order and peace, and is destructive to the virtue and character of all who indulge in it. Every thought, word or deed helps to make up our sum of life. These are the atoms that form our character; these are the seeds we sow for futurity, and the consequences of these we shall reap, and for these lament or rejoice.

DEVOTION TO GOD.

In the formation of a Guide for the youthful mind, the whole of the being must be included —the body and soul. It is the welfare of the natural or temporal that is sought, and no less the peace and prosperity of the spiritual.

Devotion to God is the whole duty of man; it is the law of Christ, the Son of God. "And thou shalt love the Lord thy God, with all thine heart, and with all thy soul, and with all thy might."—Deut. vi., 5.

Devotion is the offspring of love, without which no action can be done with sincere motives to do good. Without this, the soul must die; without it, man to God must always be a stranger; without, heaven would be a wilderness.

The more we exercise the feeling of love, of gratitude, of submission toward God, the more intense will our devotion become. It is not enough to think and talk of devotion, but we should perform devotional services. We should devote every faculty of soul and body to God, in doing good.

"Obedience to the will of God, thankfulness for His mercies, trust in His Providence, reliance on His power, and sorrow for our sins, should not be the occasional exercise, but the habit of our souls."

"The more perfectly our will is subjected to the will of God, and our whole course of conduct regulated by His commands, the more ardent will be our devotion."

OBEDIENCE.

Obedience is considered by all people as a very necessary qualification. Indeed, it is not confined to age. Among all civilized people, those who are obedient to the laws of the land, and subject to good government, are accounted more honorable than the disobedient.

The Scriptures enjoin strict obedience. "The willing and obedient shall eat the good of the land." There is no promise without obedience.

SELF-CONCEIT.

There may be passions and propensities more directly sinful, which being more apparent, are shunned on that account.

Self-conceit is a fruitful soil for every evil plant. It leads into by and forbidden paths. It releases all feelings of restraint against the passions of human nature. Under the influence of this spirit, it would be difficult to receive admonition, warning or instruction. No solemn reflection can enter the mind where it rests, no heavenly sensation can find room where it reigns.

IMPORTANCE OF
FIXED PRINCIPLES.

Without some definite and fixed principles to govern our conduct, to enable us to decide before we act,—how we should act; before we speak,—how we should speak, and what we should say, we are left like a ship upon the ocean without a pilot or rudder, and subject to be dashed upon the rocks.

It is necessary to begin early to lay the foundation of fixed principles of virtue. Without this in possession, and an obedience to the same, it is in vain for any person to obtain or to keep a good character.

To act on fixed principles should be our daily care. These extend into all the little incidents of life, and may be classed as follows;—

Of Thoughts.

Never indulge in thinking of that which is base, licentious or mean. Shun the very appearance of evil.

Of Words.

Always speak the truth, whether in earnest or in jest. Speak little and hear much. Speak no ill of any, unless necessity requires it, and then with all possible caution, doing as we would be done by. Use no hard words but let our words be mild. The fear of God should attend to all we say.

Of Actions.

Always, in all cases, obey the dictates of conscience. Do nothing that we know to be wrong, though we may gain much as a reward. Never retaliate an injury received, but render good for evil. Do nothing willingly, to injure the character of others. Always do as we would be done by. Neglect no opportunity to do good.

Always keep good promises, and make no bad ones. This inspires confidence, and without confidence man is without friends. Never promise more than we can perform, as rash promises are often the cause of neglect of punctuality. Before we resolve upon an action, cultivate the habit of deciding upon its moral character. The first question should be,—Is it right?

When we are in doubt whether a thing we would do, be wrong or right, unless obliged to do it, we would better leave it undone.

Devote time exclusively to self-examination. Weigh our actions carefully. Put ourselves in the place of those around us, and put others in our place, and remark how we would then consider our actions. If we have wronged others, and restitution be in our power, make it without hesitation.

BENEVOLENCE.

"Kindness and good-will to men should be an active characteristic of every mind. The individual who looks exclusively for self-interest, is but a rough and uncomely link in the chain of civilized society. We should ever be willing to extend to others the same privileges and blessings, which we would wish to enjoy."

Benevolence seeks to alleviate the pangs of suffering humanity,—to comfort the afflicted, and to lighten the burden of a friend, when it is too cumbrous for him to bear. The "Golden Rule" comprehends the law of benevolence and not only is it our privilege to assist others in their necessity, but it is our imperious duty so to do.

Let this principle actuate us in our relations with the world through life, and our actions will be approved be our own conscience, and by our God. Remember, that if we would be respected and beloved by our friends, and the world at large, the inestimable gem of benevolence must be kept bright by active exercise.

Wherever an opportunity offers, always lend a helping hand, or a word of sympathy. Little acts of benevolence are appreciated, and often indelibly stamped upon the mind of the receiver. Manifest this toward the aged and infirm, and in this way, lay up treasures in the kingdom of God. Possibly we may reach an advanced age, and may need corresponding care. Never take advantage of the weakness of others. If in mind, pity them; if in age, have a considerate care which it would be creditable to make public.

HONESTY.

"The strict principles of honesty and integrity should begin to be laid in the earliest days of childhood."

"There is a peace and tranquility that never slumbers in the minds of those who have strictly practiced through life, honest integrity and uprightness of dealing, which the knavish and dishonest never know."

"The former are never burdened with those

pangs of conscience to which the latter must be subjected. The honest citizen of any class or grade, holds up his head in the full congregation, standing nobly upon his own integrity and good reputation. However, his abilities or deficiencies may be criticized, here is one bulwark that is invulnerable. When weighed in the balance of judgment, he may have short-comings and imperfections, but he has never wronged the rich or poor. He knows it, and they know it."

"Upon him the widow and fatherless and the down-trodden, cast no reproaches. He has injured no man in person or property. In health or sickness, in joy or tribulation, this reflection abides with him in life, supports him through the vale of death, and exists with him beyond the tomb."

"Persons who have from early life, taken this honorable course, are often shocked and pained, especially, in later years, by seeing and hearing the sad, disgraceful end of many of their old companions who have early inclined to dishonesty."

"The pilferer has become a ruffian and a confirmed thief, and ends his career in the penitentiary or on the gallows. The knave has become a hard-hearted swindler, a pirate, or an outlaw. Those who would steal from an orchard, cheat their companions, or make false returns when sent on errands, have been turned adrift as unworthy, dishonest apprentices or pilfering clerks in pecuniary want, and with a ruined reputation."

"Those who would be knavish in trading, even in things of trifling worth, have fallen to be gamblers with all the loathsome train of vices that follow in their trail."

"Many who have sought and found the path of uprightness, and have from the morning of childhood, labored to walk in honesty and punctuality, have laid the foundation of an entirely different character. Upon this character they have stood and surveyed such wrecks of humanity, in the meridian of life, with souls filled with sorrow for those who were once dear to them, yet grateful to heaven for their own protection from the small beginnings, which result in so much misery and degradation."

PRAYER.

"Ask, and ye shall receive; seek, and ye shall find; knock, and it shall be opened unto you."

A soul that is devoted to God will not neglect to pray to Him. Let us seek His mercy in humble prayer, in silent prayer, in secret prayer, often and fervently.

"Prayer is the natural dictate of the heart. Though it may have been neglected by the careless, yet men are prompted by an irresistible impulse, to address their voice to heaven."

One of our early ministers has said,—"Let every breath be a continual prayer to God." It makes little difference whether a person is engaged in manual labor, or in silent meditation, he should give his heart to God.

CIVILITY.

Those in every rank in society will find a profitable employment in the cultivation of a refined and civil address. All who attend to it strictly, will derive great pleasure in observing how rapidly it will draw them universal respect. Among companions, this labor will crown us with many a smile of approbation.

"If we should be abused by any one, our courage should prompt us to act the manly part, and prefer to be called cowardly, rather than to disgrace ourselves by a quarrel. We must resign ourselves to this course, to be thoroughly civil and honorable."

"This discipline will perfect the habit of self-government, and render us strong under trials, and master of our nervous energies and passions. We will in the turmoil of life, present such a character; nor will madness or uncivil language ruffle our serene, peaceful deportment. Such a spirit will be sure to be seen and appreciated, even by those who, for want of reflection, have not at first rewarded and honored it."

"If we are cultivating true civility, we shall never be meanly inquisitive respecting the concerns of others. This honorable spirit will ever prompt us to attend strictly to our own business. If we are not so well provided with the blessings of this life as many others, we shall early learn to make reconciliation and philosophy take the place of fine garments and luxurious fare."

"If we address others in this spirit, we shall notice that we will be certain to please. Make the best attempts at the most civil method of utterance, and if our language is not well selected, our listeners will, at once, observe that it is deficiency and not intention. Our dependent spirit will recommend us to their respect and charity."

"If reproved for deficiencies by a friend, and even moved to tears, or disconcerted and confused; offer a brief, reasonable explanation in a quiet manner, and it will generally give ample satisfaction. Such a deportment will compromise matters, and do much to improve and elevate us."

MODESTY.

The well-bred are always modest. To be pure in spirit one should be modest in thought, word and deed. The virtue of modesty should extend to all the walks of life.

Jesus said, "Blessed are the pure in heart, for they shall see God." The immodest can not be pure in heart. The telling of obscene stories is very immodest. Purity is the teacher of modesty.

MEEKNESS AND HUMILITY.

These are essential qualifications in the character. Solomon says, "The fear of the Lord is the instruction of wisdom, and before honor is humility."—Prov. xv., 33. Remember the words of Jesus, "Whosoever exalteth himself, shall be abased, and he that humbleth himself, shall be exalted."—Luke xiv., 11.

It is natural for man to aim at self-exaltation, to be held in high estimation among mankind, and to be superior to others. The spirit of humility will prove a great treasure to the soul. It will yield the "peaceable fruits of righteousness."

RESIGNATION.

It is a matter of importance, that all learn to endure with patience and calm resignation, all crosses and unavoidable trials. We ought never to mar our happiness by our impatience. It is much better to consider that our situation is not so bad as it might be, that many others are in a much worse condition. Let us count up all of the privileges and enjoyments, and think of them instead of pondering upon the crosses and troubles, and learn to bless God for all his goodness.

CALUMNY.

Evil-speaking and backbiting are among the worst of evils. Retire from the evil speaker, and let us close the mouth, eyes and ears to this unpleasant spirit.

"We ought never to think ill of any one until we have positive proof. We should attend to our own business, and not interfere with the affairs of others, unless requested. We should equally disdain to relate, or to hear slander. The receiver is as bad as the thief."

"Look on slanderers as direct enemies to civil society, as persons without honor, honesty or humanity. Whoever entertains us with the faults of others may design to serve us in a similar manner."

CHOICE OF COMPANY.

We should endeavor, as much as possible, to keep good company, for we shall be held in estimation, according to the company we keep. The mind like the body partakes of the dispositions of the company we have chosen. It is not possible to maintain a good disposition and associate with bad company.

Those who contradict, and make every assertion a matter of dispute, betray a want of acquaintance with good manners. He, therefore, who wishes to appear amiable with those before whom he converses, will be cautious of his expressions.

Let us submit our opinion to that of others. We should look at a person when we speak to him. If we should desire to repeat what we have said, we should not raise the voice, in the repetition, lest we be thought angry.

IDLE TALK.

"We should be careful how we tell in one company, what we see or hear in another. Never divert the present company, at the expense of the last."

"In conversation, it is the general expectation of those with whom we converse, that what they say will not be repeated. Whispering in company makes the season very unpleasant. It seems to insinuate, either that the persons who we would wish should not hear, are unworthy of our confidence, or it may lead them to suppose we are speaking improperly of them; on both accounts, therefore, abstain from it."

SPEECH.

"There is an awkwardness of speech, that should and may be guarded against, such as forgetting names, and mistaking one name for another. It is the same to begin a story, without being able to finish it,—breaking off before it is finished, with,—"I have forgotten the rest of it."

Our voice and manner of speech should be cultivated. Some mumble their words, and are not intelligible; others speak so fast as not to be understood. Some talk so loudly that it might be supposed we were deaf, while others talk in scarcely more than an audible whisper. These habits should be corrected.

Avoid the use of vulgar language, and slang phrases. Such manner of speech is the distinguishing mark of a bad education. We should study to speak and to write in the best language we can command, that we may not be forced to blush at our own crudeness, when we are in company.

FORGIVENESS.

"For if ye forgive men their trespasses, your heavenly Father will also forgive you. But if ye forgive not men their trespasses, neither will your Father forgive your trespasses."

There are none so perfect but that they sometimes err, and need the forgiveness of God and of their fellow-beings. He who will not forgive a trespass, is unfitted for good society.

Whatever perfections we may have, be assured people will find them out. We should be particularly careful not to speak of personalities if we can avoid it. The less we say of ourselves, the more credit the world will give us.

HABITS.

"Avoid awkward habits. From our own observation, we should reflect what a disagreeable impression an awkward address, a slovenly figure, an ungraceful manner of speaking, whether fluttering, muttering or drawling, make upon us at first sight in strangers, and how they prejudice us against them."

We should obtain the discipline while at home, and in this way save our company much unpleasantness. We should not play with our hat, handkerchief or fingers, bite our nails, scratch our head, make a drumming sound with our feet, or have sudden fits of blowing the nose, or of coughing to clear the throat.

"This awkwardness may follow us to the table. Some sit at so great a distance from the table, that they drop food between the plate and the mouth, which may fall into the lap, or to the floor. Some hold the knife, fork or spoon very awkwardly. They grasp the knife as a carpenter would a chisel, and in this same manner use the fork, as the food is carried to the mouth."

"If they carve they do not hit the joint, but attempt to cut through the solid bone, much to the annoyance of the company. These things may not be criminal, but they should be avoided by every one who would wish to please."

ORNAMENTS OF YOUTH.

Dr. Watts on writing of education, remarked, —"Among all the accomplishments of youth, there is none preferable to a decent and agreeable behavior among men, a modest freedom of speech, a soft and elegant manner of address, a graceful and lovely deportment, a cheerful gravity and good humor, with a mind appearing ever serene under the ruffling accidents of human life. Add to this a pleasing solemnity and reverence when the discourse turns upon anything sacred and divine."

"A becoming neglect of injuries, a hatred of calumny and slander, a habit of speaking well of others, a pleasing benevolence and readiness to do good to mankind, and special compassion to the miserable. With this, an air and countenance, in a natural and unaffected manner, expressive of all these excellent qualifications."

A WORD OF CAUTION.

"Do not go needlessly, in the way of temptation. A needless indulgence and fondness for controversy upon religious subjects, with subtle men, who lie in wait to deceive, has too often exposed young Christians, and shaken their faith."

"Common, plain Christians should rather abstain from such conferences, as will fill the mind with cavils against the Scriptures, and objections against the gospel."

"A witty scoff, thrown out against the truth, may pierce the mind deeper, and stick longer than a solid argument to support the truth."

"If the Providence of God calls us into an infected house, and evident duty require us to venture our life in the midst of the pestilence, we may humbly hope for divine preservation and security. But if we venture without a call, we have reason to dread the event."

"A sincere and humble Christian may be led by the course of his duty into such dangerous company, and he may hope for the assistance of the Spirit, and the grace of God to fill his mouth with arguments, and enable him to defend his faith with holy skill and courage."

"But if he mingle himself in such sort of conversation at every turn without an evident call of Providence and from a presumption of the strength of his own faith or arguments, he has but little reason to hope for divine protection from these dangerous and fatal snares."

"Maintain a solemnity of spirit, and a serious temper of mind, in all our enquiries and discourses on a theme of such lasting importance. God and souls and eternity are no trivial ideas. It is no ludicrous matter to treat or discourse of them."

"If we have any solicitude for the honor and preservation of the gospel; if we have any tender concern for the souls of posterity, and the eternal happiness of the rising age, we should use our utmost endeavors to plant the seeds of Christianity in children, and to propagate the faith of Christ in the next generation."

"Watch against every temptation to apostasy from the Christian faith, and endeavor to guard our friends against seducers."

Be guarded, not only against the gross evils of life, but against the lesser evils. The little foxes spoil the vines. Little evils indulged, give license to greater, and these will plunder and ravage regardless of any law but passion.

"There are numerous ways in which we are exposed to go astray. Some, though they seem less important, are of very great consequence. As the loss of a small pin in a machine may render the whole useless, so the neglect of a small duty may prove our ruin."

A second is a short space of time, but without it there are no centuries. The acorn is a small nut, but from it grows the sturdy oak. The fibre of wool is small, but numbers of them clothe the sheep, and without the single fibre, the coat could not be formed. Even so every thought, word and action is a fibre which aids to form the character, either for good or evil.

Gen. George Washington's Rules for
Civility and Decent Behavior, as
published by Prof. Sparks.

1. Every action in company ought to be with some sign of respect to those present.

2. In the presence of others, sing not to yourself with a humming voice, nor drum with the fingers or feet.

3. Speak not when others speak, sit not when others stand, and walk not when others stop.

4. Turn not your back to others, especially in speaking; jog not the table or desk on which another reads or writes; lean not on any one.

5. Be no flatterer, neither play with any one that delights not to be played with.

6. Read no letters, books or papers in company; but when there is a necessity for doing so, you must not leave.

7. Come not near the books or writings of any one so as to read them unasked; also look not nigh when another is writing a letter.

8. Let your countenance be pleasant, but in serious matters somewhat grave.

9. Show not yourself glad at the misfortune

of another, though he were your enemy.

10. They that are in dignity or office have in all places precedency; but while they are young, they should respect those that are their equals in birth and other qualities, though they have no public charge.

11. It is good manners to prefer those to whom we speak before ourselves, especially if they be above us, with whom in no sort we ought to begin.

12. Let your discourse with men of business be short and comprehensive.

13. In visiting the sick do not presently play the physician, if you be not knowing therein.

14. In writing or speaking give to every person his due title according to his degree and custom of the place.

15. Strive not with your superiors in argument, but always submit your judgment to others with modesty.

16. Undertake not to teach your equal in the art he himself professes; it savors of arrogancy.

17. When a man does all he can, though it succeed not well, blame not him that did it.

18. Being to advise or reprehend any one, consider whether it ought to be in public or in private, presently, or at some other time; also on what terms to do it, and in reproving show no signs of choler, but do it with sweetness and mildness.

19. Mock not nor jest at anything of importance; break no jests that are sharp or biting; and if you deliver anything witty or pleasant, abstain from laughing thereat yourself.

20. Wherein you reprove another be unblamable yourself, for example is more prevalent than precept.

21. Use no reproachful language against any one, neither curses nor revilings.

22. Be not hasty to believe flying reports to the disparagement of any one.

23. In your apparel be modest and endeavor to accommodate nature rather than procure admiration.

24. Play not the peacock, looking everywhere about you to see if you are well decked, if your shoes fit well, if your stockings sit neatly, and clothes handsomely.

25. Associate yourself with men of good quality if you esteem your own reputation, for it is better to be alone than in bad company.

26. Let your conversation be without malice or envy, for it is a sign of a tractable and commendable nature; and in all causes of passion admit reason to govern.

27. Be not immodest in urging your friend to discover a secret.

28. Utter not base and frivolous things when among grown and learned men, nor very difficult subjects among the ignorant, nor things hard to be believed.

29. Speak not of doleful things in time of mirth nor at the table; speak not of melancholy things, as death and wounds; and if others mention them, change if you can, the discourse.

30. Break not a jest when none take pleasure in mirth.

31. Laugh not aloud, nor at all without occasion.

32. Deride no man's misfortune, though there seem to be some cause.

33. Speak not injurious words neither in jest

nor earnest.

34. Scoff at none although they give occasion.

35. Be not forward, but friendly and courteous,—the first to salute, hear and answer, and be not pensive when it is time to converse.

36. Detract not from others, but neither be excessive in commanding.

37. Go not thither where you know not whether you shall be welcome or not.

38. Give not advice without being asked; and when desired, do it briefly.

39. Reprehend not the imperfections of others, for that belongs to parents, masters and superiors.

40. If two contend together, take not the part of either unconstrained, and be not obstinate in your opinion; in things indifferent be of the major side.

41. Gaze not on the marks or blemishes of others, and ask not how they came.

42. What you may speak in secret to your friend, deliver not before others.

43. Speak not in an unknown tongue in company, but in your own language; and that, as

those of quality do, and not as the vulgar. Sublime matters treat seriously.

44. Think before you speak; pronounce not imperfectly, nor bring out your words too hastily, but orderly and distinctly.

45. When another speaks be attentive yourself, and disturb not the audience. If any hesitate in his words, help him not nor prompt him, without being desired; interrupt him not, nor answer him till his speech be ended.

46. Make no comparisons; and if any of the company be commended for any brave act of virtue, commend not another for the same.

47. Be not apt to relate news if you know not the truth thereof. In discoursing of things you have heard, name not your author always.

48. Treat with men at fit times about business, and whisper not in the company of others.

49. Be not curious to know the affairs of others, neither approach to those that speak in private.

50. Undertake not what you can not perform, but be careful to keep your promise.

51. When you deliver a matter do it without

passion and indiscretion, however mean the person may be to you.

52. When your superiors talk to anybody, hear them; neither speak nor laugh.

53. In disputes be not so desirous to overcome as not to give liberty to each one to deliver his opinion, and submit to the judgment of the major part, especially if they are judges of the dispute.

54. Be not tedious in discourse; make not many digressions, nor repeat often the same matter of the discourse.

55. Speak no evil of the absent, for it is unjust.

56. Be not angry at table, whatever happens; put on a cheerful countenance, especially if there be strangers, for good humor makes one dish a feast.

57. Set not yourself at the upper end of the table; but if it be your due, or the master of the house will have it so, contend not, lest you should trouble the company.

58. When you speak of God or his attributes, let it be seriously, in reverence and honor, and

obey your natural parents.

59. Let your recreations be manful,—not sinful.

60. Labor to keep alive in your breast, that little spark of celestial fire, called conscience.

NEEDFUL COUNSEL.

"He that hearkeneth unto counsel, is wise."

"Whoever would live long and happy, let him observe the following rules;—

Let your thoughts be rational, solid, godly.

Let your conversation be little, useful, true.

Let your conduct be profitable, virtuous, charitable.

Let your manners be sober, courteous, cheerful.

Let your diet be temperate, wholesome, sober.

Let your apparel be frugal, neat, comely.

Let your sleep be moderate, quiet, seasonable.

Let your recreations be lawful, brief, seldom.

Let your prayers be short, devout, sincere."

"Hear and learn to be silent. Be silent and learn to understand. Understand and learn to remember. Remember and learn to do accordingly."

"All that you see, judge not. All that you hear, believe not. All that you know, tell not. All that you can do, do not."

"Goods lost, some lost; courage lost, much lost; honor lost, more lost; soul lost, all lost."

"By giving alms, you lose not. By being unjust, you enrich not. By falsehood, you profit not."

Impartially examine your own failings, and meddle as little as possible with the failings of others.

"If ever you speak anything, think first, and look narrowly, what you speak, where you speak, of whom you speak, and to whom you speak; lest you bring yourself into great trouble."

Strive more to gain useful knowledge, than to show it.

Weigh the injuries you receive, and those you commit, in the same balance.

If a word spoken by your friend should offend your delicacy, avoid a hasty reply.

Always shun such things as you consider to be disagreeable in others.

Never use more freedom with children, than you are willing they should use with you, and for conscience's sake, never teach them that which is wrong.

Avoid all language that has a double meaning. It may sometimes prove very embarrassing.

If you borrow a book, return it to the owner, as soon as you have read it. If you should wish to retain it longer than propriety would suggest, you should have this understood. Never loan a borrowed book to another person.

IN PLACES CONCECRATED TO DIVINE WORSHIP.

Always take off the hat on entering the door, and have a reverential regard for the place.

"Walk softly while passing up or down the aisle."

If the assembly unitedly sit or stand, unite with them if able in body.

"If you enter a church as a stranger, wait near the door of entrance till some one comes to conduct you to a seat."

"A stranger will not enter a pew, whether occupied or not, without an invitation from some one."

Whispering should be avoided as much as possible, while laughing at what may be seen or heard, would be decidedly improper.

Attend diligently to the words of the speaker, that you may retain them in memory for future reference. The theology entertained by the worshipers may not be fully in accord with your views. You have willingly entered the house of worship, and whether the forms and ceremonies be those of a Christian, a Jew or a Pagan, it is your duty to give respectful attention. Each member thinks his form the best, and his belief the only safe passport to happiness in the future world. Even the snake worshipers of New Mexico, who may seem to be barbarians, are as fully entitled to your best attention, as would be the Bishop in a cathedral.

Speak not in time of worship of things common or domestic, or of anything foreign from the duty of the occasion.

"If you enter a church through curiosity, when the worshipers are not present, be as respectful as on the Sabbath."

"There are many sects; they reverence their religion. Many among them are sincerely attached to their own forms and order of worship. If there is anything dear to man and woman, in which they should be protected, it is the conscientious manner they select to worship God."

"Let the worshiper be considered by the mass, never so erroneous, if his exercises are harmless, this right should be sacredly secured to him by every just law and civil obligation. If there is any change in his ideas or creed, he should make it himself, as he obtains higher light and a more correct understanding."

"He who delights in disturbing the general peace of society, cultivates a lawless disposition."

"The sacrilegious person who disturbs the house of worship, and wounds the feelings of the worshipers, will do more than this; he will prove a disturber of other public gatherings."

GENERAL BEHAVIOR BEFORE ALL PERSONS.

We should always respect the aged and infirm, and never retain a seat when they stand for the want of one. Always be kind to them, through care and attention, and assist in making their advanced years, pleasant and agreeable.

When walking with those who are elder in years, always give them the right hand.

Always show deference to those who are elder, when in company, and never, carelessly, push by them. Never contradict them, even though we may think they are in error.

When three persons walk together, the center place is considered the most honorable, and a son may properly walk at the right hand of his father, while a younger brother walks at the left hand.

Place should be given to those who excel us, whether in quality, age or learning.

"A gentleman will always remove his hat upon entering a dwelling."

Walk easily across the floor, and do not slam the doors.

Always thank a person who does or offers a kindness.

"In asking a favor say;—If you please, and when it is granted,—say;—I thank you."

If we wish to receive a kindness of others, it is not proper to enquire about their business, or whether they are in a hurry; but ask them kindly for their assistance, and if they can not oblige us, let them make their own excuses."

Reprove easily and modestly, if duty require it, especially when wicked actions or indecent expressions are brought forward.

Always be punctual.

In speaking of others in company with ourselves, always mention their names first.

Always knock at the door of a private room

before entering.

Never call nicknames. It is a vulgar way of showing what we dare to do.

"Avoid telling stories in company, unless they are short and applicable to the subject under consideration."

Never take a story from another person, because you think you can tell it better.

In coughing or sneezing make as little noise as consistent.

"Avoid yawning, lounging, rubbing the face or chin, with the hand, or fidgeting, while in company."

If yawning can not be avoided, place a kerchief before the mouth.

Never refuse a gift that is offered in kindness, but acknowledge its receipt immediately.

"To answer a person impatiently, is not only unkind, but a lack of true politeness."

To treat others unkindly, is to demean ourselves.

"Some persons are very absent-minded in company. They give but slight attention to what is being said. Some are whispering much of the time, and such persons make themselves very objectionable to those who are present."

Never speak diminutively of any one in company. Better wait a suitable time, and then give the needed admonition.

If those of our own age do anything amiss, while in company, we should never excuse ourselves, and blame others.

When we treat a company to food, fruit, or drink, always treat the Elders of the company first. If strangers are present, wait first on them.

The teeth should receive careful attention.

"Avoid dirty finger nails."

Especial care should be taken of borrowed books. To turn down the leaves, make marks on the margin with a pencil or pen, for special reference, or to soil the print with unwashed hands, is, to say the least, a sad lack of careful discipline.

Never enter the workshops of strangers without liberty, nor interfere with the machinery or tools; nor ask unnecessary questions of merchants about the prices of articles which we do not intend to purchase.

·⚜·

As too much care can not be exercised in regard to the rules of good behavior, we will, in a little more familiar style, enlarge on this one special subject that claims so much of our attention.

THE SITTING POSTURE.

Teacher. To be able to meet the approbation of cultivated minds does not require us to live among the wealthy, nor to stand with those in high official position. Those who are poor in the treasures of this world, may become as cultivated and as graceful in manners, as those who reside in a palace. Personal discipline belongs to every one who would make himself agreeable in society.

Whether at home or abroad, we are, a greater part of our time, cultivating habits that will become more or less permanent, and which we shall manifest in the society of those whom we may have occasion to visit. The influence which this exerts on the mind is second only to the language which may be used by the individual.

A. Allow me to ask,—What position should I occupy while sitting in a chair?

B. I do not see why I can not sit in a chair as I may choose!

Teacher. While your position in sitting should be free and natural, it should also represent the self-respect which you entertain for your own mind. If the company is under any particular order of discipline, by all means conform to the regulations, or politely withdraw. A variation from this rule would indicate either a careless habit or a diseased state of the body. To do as B. says, you should keep company with clowns, or with those who do not study to become agreeable in good society. It is very unkind to oblige others to accept our awkwardness and indolence.

A. I think it is easier to sit forward in a chair, or let it fall against the wall, than to sit erect.

B. The chairs are all too low or too high, and

I want to tip back, anyhow.

C. I do not think the trouble is in the chair. B. has just moved from the city, and he says that is the way city people do.

Teacher. Possibly many in the city and many out of the city may practice the same awkward habits. All well ordered society must have some rules of discipline, or it would soon return to a very low order of life. You tell me that you are studying the laws of hygiene, and that they teach you to sit erect; that the habit of leaning forward while writing or reading or conversing, is very injurious, and produces weakness of the spine; that the practice of sliding forward in the chair, also produces the same results. Why do you not profit by your study? While we would not like to see you all gauged, sitting bolt upright, all the time, which course would be neither graceful nor sociable, we would not like to have you show such undue familiarity in the use of your legs, as to bring a blush upon the company.

B. If I have a rocking chair I can rock, can't I?

Teacher. If you are privileged to sit in a rocking chair, you should endeavor to conform to the general custom of the company,—but chairs without rockers should always rest their four posts upon the floor. The man who left his invited guests in the parlor, to get a piece of board to place under the chair of one of the party, was a wise man. Should you happen to sit in a chair that is too low for your comfort, excuse yourself and respectfully ask for one that is higher.

D. I think we sometimes tip our chairs back against the wall, and then place our feet on the rounds which mars the paint and injures the furniture.

B. Can't we do anything? What is the use of being so particular?

Teacher. If you are unable to sit properly in company, you should practice a system of daily discipline till you are able to do so. It is very rude to deface the property of your friends, and poor economy to injure your own. The chair will be liable to break the plastering if it is forced against it. Your feet should never touch the furniture, and your hands should be kept from it as much as is consistent.

B. Well, I'm glad I'm not obliged to be in company all of the time!

Teacher. You are never alone.

B. I mean when I go to the workshop, or am about my daily employment; then I can sit or stand as I please.

Teacher. Too many already allow themselves to be careless and indifferent about the cultivation of their manners while at home, anticipating that when in company, it is only necessary to be particular, and conduct with grace and propriety. Such a course often results in some scene of mortification to the individual or perhaps to all who may be present. Habits which are cherished in private can not be laid off like a cloak on appearing in company.

Consider yourself in the company of your friends at all times, and so act and converse that you will not be obliged to practice an affected style. If you allow yourself to tip back in a delicately made chair which is without rockers, you are liable to break it. Such chairs are not intended for rough use. If you do not injure the chair, you may cut holes through the carpet or deface the floor.

A. I wonder if anybody observed how I was sitting, last evening, while in company with those friends?

Teacher. What was your position?

A. Extremely awkward, I guess, and I wish now that I had stayed away. How ashamed I am! I did exactly wrong in almost everything. Instead of sitting erect, I slid forward in my chair, and pushed my feet out quite a distance.

C. At one time I found that I had my feet on the rounds of the chair.

B. While I was waiting a few moments, I found that I was carelessly twirling a chair on one of its legs. I hope it was not observed as I should be sorry to have them call me a clown.

Teacher. Really, what a life picture you have drawn! All that you have said, and more, has frequently come under my observation. You need to practice a little more self-discipline or your friends will be obliged to suffer an ill-timed pennance when you are present.

Do not place your feet by the side of your

chair and every few minutes catch hold of your clothing to raise your feet from the floor. Some persons remind us of the old-fashioned "fulling-mill,"—out goes one foot as far as it can be extended from the body. In a few minutes that foot is drawn back, and out goes the other foot, and so they alternately, play back and forth.

Have a care for those knees; they are sadly distanced from each other for respectable society. An Indian sitting on the floor would appear more gracefully. Whatever position you may take, study to be graceful. Have as much thought for the comfort and pleasure of your friends, as you have for your own personal or selfish interest. You can not be too particular in this respect, whether at home or abroad.

·❧❀❧·

CONVERSATION.

In conversation, have special care lest we wound the tender feelings of our friends. We should remember that jests and jokes are like edged tools, and very dangerous to use.

Quietness in all things is essential to a well ordered person. He shuns all outward display of personality. His voice is low, his words simple and his actions grave.

Carefully avoid placing anything to the mouth while speaking.

A fetid breath may cause some of our listeners, suddenly to retire.

In addressing a person, speak not without some title of respect, which is due to him, or if he have an official title, neglect not to use it.

Conversation can not be carried on, very pleasantly, by one person. If one does the talking, while the other is continually saying,—yes, yes;—yes, yes—or—just so,—or—yes, I see,—it becomes stupid in the extreme. If we expect to be present in company, we should make ourselves familiar with a few names of the prominent men and women, and then commit to memory the names of three or four authors, and with these do our best. Have in mind some little incident, as referring to one or more of them. Even this trivial knowledge will "cover a multitude of our sins," of ignorance.

"Boast not, in discourse, of our wit, or of what we may have done."

It is a trespass upon the manners of good society to question the truthfulness of an assertion, while with others in conversation.

"In meeting persons always turn to the right."

"A gentleman should go up stairs before a lady, and behind her in coming down."

It is rude to stare at people in company.

"On entering a house, a gentleman or gentlemanly boy will remove his hat, and never allow it upon his head inside the door."

"When in company it is not the place to carry on a personal or private conversation."

If we can not give respectful attention while in company, we would better remain at home.

Whistling, drumming with the hands or feet, or going to the windows to see who is passing, is not a good representation of careful manners.

We should keep step with the person with whom we are walking.

"Many of the early habits of courtesy or rudeness will cling to us through life."

In all our conversation it is well to use the

best language we can command. Speak distinctly, in plain English. Avoid all slang phrases, all profanity and all expressions that have a doubtful meaning.

We should avoid the habit of laughing at everything we have to say.

"Many persons who have a correct knowledge of the rules of grammar can not utter a phrase without betraying a coarseness of speech."

"Avoid speaking of any of our private affairs to others. If we neglect to do this, we may become disagreeable to ourselves and to them."

In proportion as we value the society of our best friends, we shall avoid the retention of decayed teeth. They are not only injurious to the general health, but the fetid breath which is forced into the face of those with whom conversation is held, is intolerable. A Christian in prayer, with an unwashed mouth, and retaining badly decayed teeth, would send up such an offering as no angel would dare touch, even with his wing.

*Regard for those with whom we
are not personally acquainted.*

Always treat strangers with civility and kindness. Give them correct information if they should enquire about any person, or the way to any place.

It is quite impolite to gaze at strangers, or to laugh at them because they appear singular.

Never stand conspicuously before the window, nor in the door, to stare at those who are passing the dwelling.

Always say, Good Morning, or Good Evening, to those whom we may meet during the day.

"Never refuse to return the salute of any person, even though he may be very clownish. Some one asked the Hon. Henry Clay, of Kentucky, why he returned the salute of a negro. His reply was,—'I never allow, even a negro, to outdo me in politeness.'"

Introducing. "The introduction of one person to another is generally, the younger to the elder, and a gentleman to a lady, and those less in station to those more advanced, as,—Mrs. Jones, allow me to introduce to you my friend, Miss Smith. Mrs. Miller, allow me the pleasure of introducing to you, my friend, Mr. Miles."

"In introducing a gentleman to a lady, address her first as—Miss Jones, permit me to introduce Mr. Lee."

"Be careful when introducing friends, to pronounce the name of each one, clearly and distinctly, that there may be no mistake."

"When there are several persons waiting for an introduction to one individual, present the latter one as first, and then in succession name the others, bowing as each name is called."

If a person of distinction is to be introduced, the official title should be used, as;—

His Excellency, Abraham Lincoln; or, His Excellency, Gov. Rollins; or, Honorable, Nathaniel E. Martin, or, Honorable, William E. Chandler.

"Many a man has gained wealth by learning to practice patience and forbearance while dealing with customers."

"Persons who are careful of their manners, will not practice eating while on the street."

"Good manners will keep us from laughing at the mistakes or accidents of others."

No one should make himself conspicuous in company, by loud laughing or talking.

Allow the person who commences a story to finish it properly, without an interruption. If we think we are better informed we should wait for a suitable time to make the statement.

"The good, are those who are educated to know, and trained to practice the rules of good morals and gentle manners."

Never allow any kissing to be done in a public place, nor with strangers, or relatives at home. This manifestation of affection in such a public manner is very questionable. Disease may be introduced in this way, that many years would fail to eradicate.

"On entering a store, we should not make unnecessary trouble for the clerks. It is crude to haggle over the price of an article. If we can not pay what is asked for it, we can leave it. If a clerk puts himself to more trouble than we have a right to expect, we must not forget to thank him."

These general principles of politeness, in stores, can be applied in all public places.

"We should consider in reference to our conduct, two things; first, the courtesy we owe to others, and second, the respect we owe to ourselves."

BEHAVIOR AT THE TABLE.

It has often been remarked, that it may be known whether a person is well-bred, or not, by seeing him eat at the dining table; therefore, it is highly necessary for all to observe the rules of good behavior, while sitting at the table.

It is essentially necessary to the happiness of a family, that a system of rules should be observed, during the time occupied in the dining hall, which will make the season one of pleasurable satisfaction, as well as of physical necessity. A slight deviation from the rules of propriety, may touch the nerves of one or more of the company so unpleasantly, that the occasion becomes one of pain instead of pleasure. To avoid this state, a strict, personal discipline must be self-imposed while in the company of others, and especially while partaking of our meals.

"It is the custom of Christian people, generally, to have some form of religious observance before eating. Whatever it may be, we should give it our respectful attention."

Many private families have a code of manners, more or less, peculiar to themselves. We should observe their customs and when consistent conform to them out of respect to the family where we are guests.

Remain perfectly quiet till the close of the ceremonies, which may be the saying of grace, the reading of a lesson, or the offering of prayer.

If the host or hostess asks our preference in regard to articles of food, a clear and concise answer should be given in the best language we can command.

Sit erect at the table, but while eating, incline the body slightly forward.

Adjust the napkin neatly, to favor personal convenience. Keep the arms near the body, that those in the adjoining seat may not be discommoded by our awkwardness.

Do not rest the elbows on the table.

Be careful not to have the feet in the way of others.

"As food does not improve by waiting, attention should be given when called to the table."

There is a proper way to handle the napkin, knife, fork and spoon. We should study to learn the correct way, and avoid an awkwardness in these little things.

"We should not forget to say, Please pass the bread, or any other dish that may be wanted."

"We should ask for an article by name, and never point to a dish."

In passing a knife, fork or spoon to others, always offer them the handle, and in presenting a pitcher, pass it with the handle toward them.

If articles of food are laid upon the personal plate, eat that which is agreeable, and forbear making any comments, or expressing likes and dislikes.

Good behavior at the table adds largely to the happiness of all who are present.

Take no observation of others while they eat, nor of the food they eat.

"Take soup from the side of the spoon, and avoid any noise."

Every movement at the table should be made with as little noise as possible.

Sit easily in the chair, neither too near the table, nor too far from it. Never play with the knife or fork.

We should neither eat nor drink in great haste. This should be avoided.

If necessary to speak while at the table, do it in a mild voice that it may not disturb others.

Do not present an untidy appearance at table. The hands and face should be clean and the hair neatly arranged.

If there by anything unpleasant in the food, or unsuitable, put it quietly aside without attracting the attention of others.

"Never seize immediately on what is liked best, at table, to the deprivation of others."

Never be putting food into the mouth, and at the same time be looking at other objects.

Never attempt to drink while food is in the mouth.

If the cup has a handle, use it while drinking; if not, clasp around the outside, but never put the fingers in the cup.

"Do not pour coffee or tea from the cup into the saucer, and do not blow either these or soup."

"After using the spoon, remove it from the cup, and allow it to remain in the saucer."

"When more coffee is desired, let the spoon remain in the saucer, but if no more is desired, allow the spoon to remain in the cup."

"The saucer should only be used as a receptacle for the cup, never to drink from."

"It is considered improper to use a knife at the table, for any other purpose than for cutting the food or spreading the bread with butter."

"Everything that can be cut without a knife,

should be cut with a fork."

"Such food as can not be eaten with a fork, should be taken up with a spoon."

"Be careful not to touch with the hands, what we do not intend to eat ourselves, whether we cut or break bread, cake, pie or any other article of food. 'Hands off' has a mannerly value in this place."

Avoid touching the hands to the head, or to any part of the body, while at the table, unless absolutely necessary.

"Never reach over the plate of another person to obtain a distant article,—better ask some one to pass it."

Never find fault with the food. If it is too hot, allow it to cool, but do not blow on it. If any article is on our plate that we do not wish to eat, place it in the dish provided for refused articles, or leave it on the side of the plate.

In social or domestic circles the needed and nice provisions are not always made for the table, and some are apt from the influence of their common habits at home, to make some wide deviations from good manners.

In order to appear well-bred at table, when in company, attention must be paid three times a day to the points of table manners. If these are neglected at home, and in private, they will be performed awkwardly when in company.

"Never, put any fish or meat bones, or stones of fruit on the table cloth, but place them on the edge of the plate."

Learn to eat an egg from the shell. It is easily done.

Corn by common usage is eaten from the cob, but the exhibition is not interesting.

Cheese should be eaten with the fork.

Always keep the mouth closed while chewing.

Have a regard for the careful moving of the chair, in taking position at the table.

Laughing and talking at the table are quite unbecoming, unless that is the custom of the family who are entertaining us.

It is quite admissible and much the better way, when sitting with strangers to be very moderate in all movements, and carefully observe the general course that is pursued by the directors of the table, whether rich or poor, and accept this as the guide.

Fruit should be cut into small pieces, before being carried to the mouth. It should never be bitten.

"Be very careful not to soil the table cloth by allowing anything to fall from the plate."

"Never return any part of the food that has been on a personal plate, to the dish."

"Break or cut bread and apply the butter as we wish to eat it. Do not bite it in mouthfuls from a large slice."

"Thoroughly masticate the food, and all audible noises, while eating should be avoided."

"Avoid making any noise in eating, even if each meal is eaten in solitude. Eat slowly. Cut all food into small pieces."

"Use the butter knife as scrupulously when alone, as if a roomful of people were watching us."

Always allow the plate to remain in its proper position on the table, and never raise it on the edge to remove the food from it.

"When eating entirely alone, it is well to observe these little details, thus making them perfectly familiar."

Avoid as far as possible, coughing or sneezing. In case of necessity turn the face from the table and cover the mouth with the napkin.

"Never blow the nose at the table, as it might unsettle the stomachs of those near. If the case becomes imperative, it would be the duty of the person to leave the table to accomplish the purpose."

Do not pick the teeth while sitting at the table, nor allow eructations to escape from the stomach during the time of eating.

The nervous system is sometimes attuned very delicately, and a person may be forced to leave the table on account of the carelessness of others.

To make any noise unnecessarily with either the lips or the nose, while eating, may be very disagreeable to those who sit near us.

Eat what is needed before rising from the table. If at a Hotel and fruit is placed on the table, we may put one article by the side of the plate, and on rising take it with us, but at a private table this should never be done except at the request of the entertainer.

If there is a delicacy on the table, partake of it sparingly.

We should not take upon our plate any more food than we may expect to eat, as it would be as wrong to waste our food, as to throw our money into the highway.

"When napkins are not provided, the handkerchief must be used as a substitute. The napkin is to be used to protect the dress from injury, and as a towel for the fingers and mouth if they become soiled. It should never be employed as a kerchief for the nose, or to remove perspiration from the face."

Believers in Community life should study a strict economy, and if they have more of the good things of this world than they need for their own use, they should give them to the poor.

Never attempt to talk, and at the same time be eating.

"Make use of the napkin if any food should soil the fingers."

These customs in society are constantly

changing in reference to many little things. Those who wish to appear to advantage, will be obliged to be self-possessed in order to observe closely, everything that is passing around them.

If an accident occurs while at the table, or any uncommon noise is made, a cultivated person will not appear to notice it.

After finishing the meal, follow the custom of the family we are in, while disposing of the knife, fork or spoon. If left upon the plate, place the handles together, the blade of the knife toward us, and let the fork rest upon the point of the tines.

When at home a system of manners should be observed at the table, and would give tone and character, and be the manifestation of a care and discipline that may prove congenial to those who are present.

A due regard for self-respect would suggest a care of the garments that are worn, and of the cleanliness of the person.

"Leave the napkin by the side of the plate, when away from home. At home we may fold it, and place the ring around it."

CLEANLINESS.

For all who desire to be considered honorable members of society, cleanliness is a very necessary accomplishment. A slovenly person is very disagreeable, especially, in well ordered company.

Cleanliness is closely conjoined to the moral law. An undisciplined mind, with coarse and low habits, would make a sorry specimen of a Christian.

It would be vain for a person to talk of purity of heart while he indulges in slovenly habits. Filthiness of person and purity of mind can never harmonize. Cleanliness of heart will show itself by good works, as really as charity or love.

A life of right thinking and acting has a great influence for good manners.

"The hands, face, neck and ears should be thoroughly washed every morning. The washing of the hands and wrists should be done much more frequently."

"The finger nails should be trimmed and always kept clean."

"The bath should not be neglected. Make use of some form of bathing frequently, both for health and cleanliness."

"An unwashed person, or one who neglects to change his under-clothing frequently will be very offensive to all with whom he converses."

"Always be provided with a clean handkerchief. It is one sure mark of a gentleman."

"Neatness in personal habits is the first mark of good discipline that attracts an observer. A sloven can not be a gentleman."

"The hair should be thoroughly brushed every morning, and the face and hands washed. Cleanliness is not promoted by the constant use of hair oil."

"An excess of perfumery on the person is not in good taste."

"No one can pleasantly entertain in company, however graceful he may be, unless he is neat and clean in his personal habits."

To spit on the floor of a dwelling, to wear muddy shoes into the halls, or badly soiled garments into any company, or neglect to wash the hands before entering the dining hall, are deviations too flagrant to need comment.

"A particular regard to the cleanliness of the mouth, teeth, hands and nails, is always demanded. We must keep them clean, especially, when in company, lest we inflict disgust and nausea on sensitive minds."

"There are some things that should receive attention in our own private room, as;—scratching the head or ears, picking the teeth, or constantly adjusting the clothing. The blowing of the nose is not a pleasant demonstration at any time, and in company or at the table it is simply unpardonable."

Be neat and clean. Dress accordingly to the occupation, and then discipline yourself to habits of neatness.

Whether our garments are new or old, adjust them to the person as well as may be consistent, and not present an untidy appearance, by carelessly throwing them upon the body.

Shoes untied, or worn in slip-shod manner, with stockings hanging loose around the ankles do not conduce to neatness of the person.

Avoid the wearing of ragged clothes, as they

induce uncleanness and laziness.

Have a place for every garment and when not in use, it should be properly put away, instead of throwing it upon the floor, or in a chair.

Avoid the habit of constantly thrusting the hands into the pockets. It is not a graceful exhibition, either in or out of company.

"It is a common saying that people generally, do not know what to do with their hands and feet. Let them take an easy position of themselves. To sit still gracefully, is an accomplishment worth acquiring."

This maxim has been verified quite often,— "He that is negligent at twenty years of age, will be a sloven at forty, and intolerable at fifty."

Cleanliness of the person is health, and health is beauty.

LETTER-WRITING.

In replying to a letter, always acknowledge the date of the letter received, also the subject matter and then write whatever may need your attention.

You should not impose on others a sheet of errors or erasures, or write so blindly as to give the impression that your letter is a puzzle. Better make a clean copy.

Study the rules of punctuation and then use them as correctly as you can while writing a letter.

A letter sheet of white paper, and written with black or blue black ink, will prove the most acceptable.

Letters written to persons in official capacity, or to strangers, should receive the best of attention in every respect.

Anonymous letters should never be written. If you are not willing to place your signature to what you have written, it should never be sent away.

Always enclose a stamp if you solicit a reply.

In folding the letter sheet, study to do it as nicely as is consistent.

Prepare the envelope with the same care as you do the letter.

Never use a postal card when there is anything private or personal to be written on it.

Take express care in the superscribing of your envelope, and place a stamp on the upper right-hand corner.

Obtain more extended rules for the writing of letters and study them carefully.